Good New[s]

Written by Lisa Thompson

Pictures by Andy Hamilton

The King told the news to the Queen.

2

3

The Queen told the news to the Prince.

The Prince told the news to the Princess.

The Princess told the news to the Knight.

The Knight gave the news to the bird.

10

11

The bird gave the news to the King.

12

13

"Good news!"
said the King.
"We are going
to a party!"

14

15